Why Voting Matters (PowerKids Press) (Library Binding)

Why Should People Vote? $17.70

This book explores how people choose a candidate to vote for and why that choice matters.

#2073968   K. Nelson   Available:08/15/2018   24 pgs
Grade:234   Dewey:324.60

Why *Voting* Matters

How Do People Vote?

Kristen Rajczak Nelson

PowerKiDS
press™

NEW YORK

Published in 2019 by The Rosen Publishing Group, Inc.
29 East 21st Street, New York, NY 10010

Editor: Elizabeth Krajnik
Book Design: Rachel Rising

Photo Credits: Cover, pp. 5, 21 Blend Images - Hill Street Studios/Brand X Pictures/Getty Images; Background, Cover, pp. 1, 3, 4, 6, 8, 10, 12, 14, 16, 18, 20, 22–24 PepinoVerde/Shutterstock.com; p. 7 asiseeit/E+/Getty Images; p. 9 iStockphoto.com/ertyo5; p. 11 Comstock Images/Stockbyte/Getty Images; p. 13 cmannphoto/E+/Getty Images; p. 15 iStockphoto.com/ YinYang; p. 17 Hero Images/Hero Images/Getty Images; p. 19 Lisa F. Young/ Shutterstock.com; p. 22 iStockphoto.com/InkkStudios.

Cataloging-in-Publication Data

Names: Rajczak Nelson, Kristen.
Title: How do people vote? / Kristen Rajczak Nelson.
Description: New York : PowerKids Press, 2019. | Series: Why voting matters | Includes index.
Identifiers: LCCN ISBN 9781538330098 (pbk.) | ISBN 9781538330074 (library bound) | ISBN 9781538330104 (6 pack)
Subjects: LCSH: Voting--United States--Juvenile literature. | Elections--United States--Juvenile literature. | Political participation--United States--Juvenile literature.
Classification: LCC JK1978.R35 2019 | DDC 324.60973--dc23

Manufactured in the United States of America

CPSIA Compliance Information: Batch #CS18PK For further information contact Rosen Publishing, New York, New York at 1-800-237-9932.

Contents

Casting a Vote

One of the most important duties of a U.S. **citizen** is voting. Voting is making an **official** choice for a government leader by casting a **ballot**. When a group votes on a leader at a certain time, it's called an election. There are elections for town and state leaders, as well as for the U.S. president!

Becoming a Voter

In order to vote, a person has to **register** by filling out a form. They can register to vote if they're a U.S. citizen who is 18 years old on or before the next Election Day. They also must be a **resident** of their state for an amount of time set by the state.

7

Can Everyone Vote?

Voters have to register so workers at **polling places** can make sure no one votes twice. Not everyone can register to vote. People who live in the United States but aren't citizens can't vote in federal elections. People who have carried out certain crimes can't vote in some states, too.

VOTE AQUI

VOTE HERE

在这里投票

Join the Party

When someone registers to vote, they often join a political party. Political parties are groups that share the same ideas about how the government should be run. The two main political parties in the United States are the Democrats and the Republicans. There are smaller political parties called third parties.

Democratic Party symbol

Republican Party symbol

11

Some Stay Independent

People join political parties to show **support** for government ideas they believe in. Sometimes, joining a political party allows them to vote in elections called **primaries**. You can also be an independent, or a person who doesn't belong to a political party. In some states, independents aren't allowed to vote in primaries.

☐ Democrat

☐ Republican

☐ Independent

Where to Be

Voters need to know where and when elections are. This information may come in the mail. A voter can also check their town or state's website for dates and times. It's important for voters to know where their local polling places are. Churches, community centers, and fire stations are often polling places.

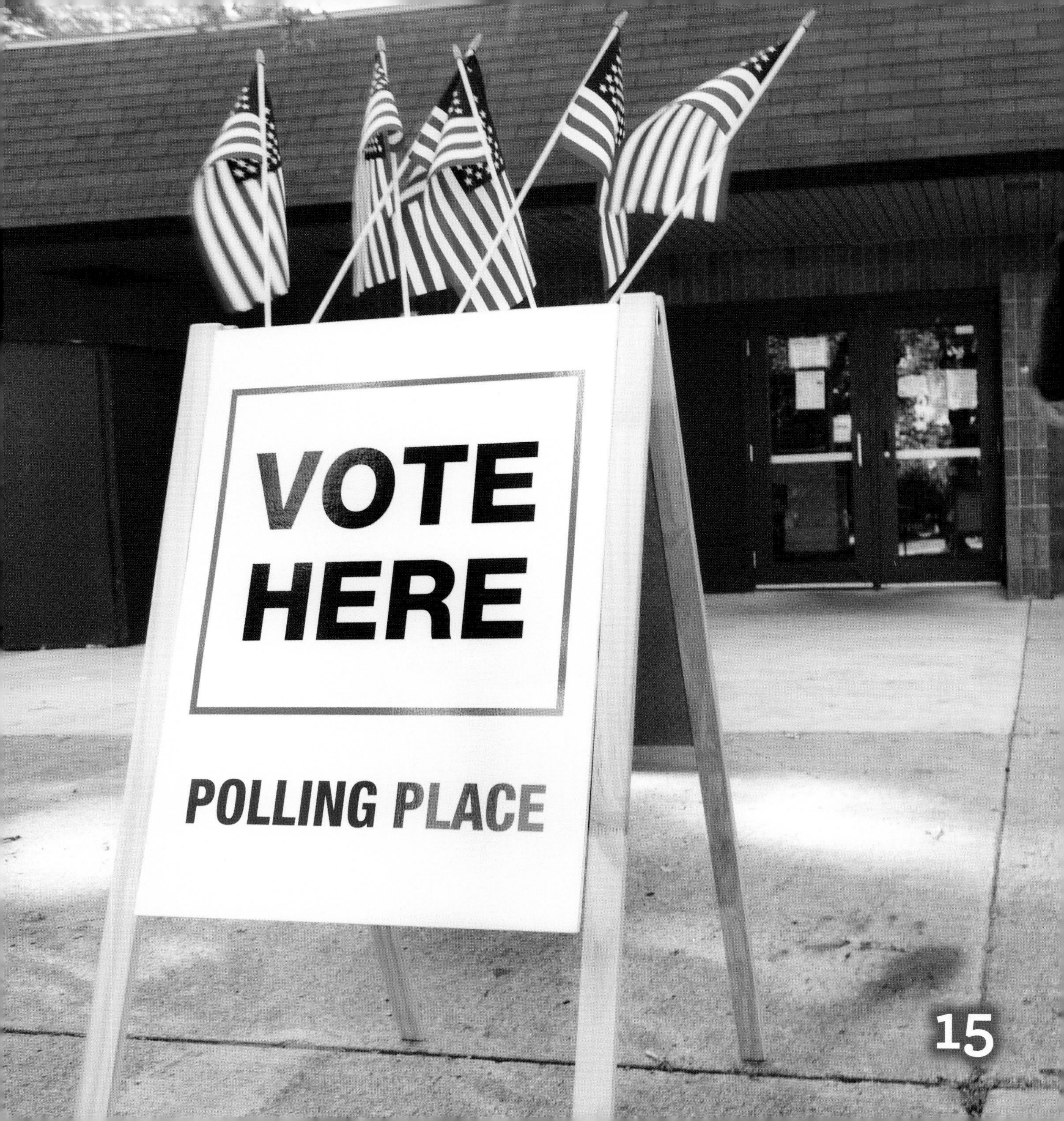
VOTE
HERE
POLLING PLACE

Bring ID

When at a polling place, voters may need to show workers a voter registration card. They may need another kind of **ID** that has their picture. What each voter needs depends on the state. In some states, voters don't need ID! They just sign next to their name in a book.

Polling Station HRO 49 Voter List

Make the Choice

Casting a ballot is different from state to state. Some states give out paper ballots and pens. Voters color in a circle next to their choice. These may be counted by hand or by a machine. Other states have voters use a special kind of computer to cast their ballot.

19

Vote from Far Away

Some states let people vote early if there's a chance they may miss the election. Members of the military, some college students, and U.S. citizens living elsewhere can also mail in a ballot called an absentee ballot. They receive their ballot before Election Day. They send it by a certain date for their vote to be counted.

Voters' Voices

No matter who's voting or where they cast their vote, all votes are cast in secret and all votes are counted. Voting gives U.S. citizens a voice in their government. Citizens have a chance to show those in power what ideas they care about—and vote for people who uphold those ideas!

Glossary

ballot: A vote cast in an election. Also a piece of paper that a vote is cast on.

citizen: A person who lives in a country and has the rights given to them by that country's laws.

ID: Identification, or an official card or piece of paper that has your name and other facts about you on it.

official: Recognized by the government or someone in power.

polling place: A building where voters go to cast their votes.

primary: An election in which members of the same political party run against each other for a chance to be in a larger and more important election.

register: To put your name on an official list.

resident: A person who lives in a place.

support: The act of showing you agree with someone or something.

Index

Websites

Due to the changing nature of Internet links, PowerKids Press has developed an online list of websites related to the subject of this book. This site is updated regularly. Please use this link to access the list: www.powerkidslinks.com/wvm/hdpv